Colourful Advent

A new way to pray when words are inadequate

Sheila Julian Merryweather

kevin mayhew

First published in 2004 by

KEVIN MAYHEW LTD
Buxhall, Stowmarket, Suffolk, IP14 3BW
E-mail: info@kevinmayhewltd.com

KINGSGATE PUBLISHING INC
1000 Pannell Street, Suite G, Columbia, MO 65201
E-mail: sales@kingsgatepublishing.com

9 8 7 6 5 4 3 2 1 0

ISBN 1 84417 273 2
Catalogue No. 1500710

Cover design by Angela Selfe
Edited by Katherine Laidler
Typesetting by Louise Selfe

Printed and bound in Great Britain

Introduction

In this book I have used colour as a means of expression of the prayer that has emerged when considering certain Advent topics. I hope that you too will enjoy using colour in this way.

Traditionally, Advent has been regarded as a time of preparation for Christmas, but how that time has been observed has varied enormously – ignored completely by some and kept with a strict adherence to rules and regulations by others.

In my early years I did not enjoy Advent. It was a time when I was made to look at subjects for which I was not ready. The topics of death, judgement and hell were very frightening and left me convinced I never would make heaven, which was supposed to be where Advent was leading. Fortunately, this hasn't been everyone's experience. Most will have realised that new life comes through death.

Now I look forward to and enjoy Advent. The emphasis has changed from doom and gloom to hope and expectancy, which I am sure is right in readiness for the coming – the Advent – of Christ: Christmas.

However, we cannot completely ignore the difficult, frightening subjects, but we can look at them with God on our side and that makes all the difference.

In our busy, non-stop world it is hard sometimes – in fact, most of the time – to realise that God is there – here – on our side.

I have been very fortunate to live for many years in the tropics – first in Sabah, Malaysia and more recently in the Solomons. In both countries one is much more aware of the seasons kept by the Church. In the jungle and then on an island, I was cut off from all the normal day-to-day interchange of news which excites and worries us. I had no shops to tempt and tease me. During those years I only knew which month and which day of the week it was by following the Church's calendar. Advent, therefore, became much more real. It was the time leading up to the end of the school year and the Christmas holiday – a time to enjoy, not dread. It became a time to prepare to receive the revelation of God. To discover more and more the vulnerability of God in Jesus, the vulnerability of God in others and, most amazing, the vulnerability of God in ourselves – in you and in me.

I invite you to come with me through each week of Advent and see if we can discover how God can help us face some of the difficult subjects that confront us.

We can do this, for Advent isn't just in the future. We have had many experiences of advents or comings in the past, even though we may not have recognised them. Advent is a 'coming' in each moment of the present. I cannot put into words how to tackle, how to receive the mysteries that surround us, but using colour helps to give expression to the experience.

These two circles or prayer symbols were both focused on Advent.

This is how I used to feel about Advent. A deep fear of death, judgement and hell. Not much hope of heaven in this one!

Later, I was still not very sure about anything – quite shaky, in fact! But the bright yellow is there – a colour which for me is a reminder that God is in all things, all events, all people, everywhere.

Hope has crept in with the blue and a new awareness comes with the green. God is there ready for all the other 'colours' to look up to.

Advent was becoming a more wholesome entity for me.

Suggestion

Before reading on, you may like to colour your Advent circle or symbol as you feel it is for you today. Don't think about the colours or be influenced by mine. Everyone's choice will be different. Just use the first colours that come to mind. They will be the right ones for you now.

My Advent symbol for today looks very different from the previous two. It includes all my colours and is no longer 'scary' – just full of the unknown that is represented by the grey. It is an inviting symbol now.

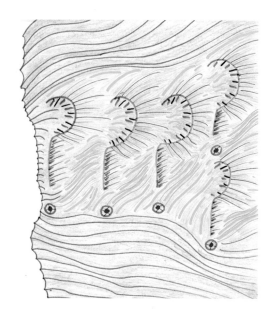

The First Week of Advent

This was the week in which, traditionally, the Church considered the subject of death.

Life is full of 'little deaths' which we have to work through, much as we would like to ignore them. For example, we fail an important examination, or we present badly at an interview and so do not get the job we had set our heart on. We lose someone we love through the break up of an engagement or when a marriage ends in divorce. The children grow up and leave home. All these and similar events give us pain. It's as though already we feel the shadow of death.

Death is a difficult subject for many of us to think about. It is not only whether we have faith enough to believe that death is a new beginning and not the end, but also whether we can accept the scary thought of growing old and of dying.

During Advent, take time to consider your own fears, for each fear causes us a little death. We need the courage to pray about such fears and then we shall find help to deal with them.

One of my own fears has been the fear of ageing. I'll share with you how I've been helped with that particular fear. It is a shock to the system when it first hits one that the process of ageing has really begun. I can still remember how appalled I felt when I suddenly became aware of all the brown patches on my hands, and later the veins all standing up creating mountains and valleys on them! Of course, many other signs have followed. How could I cope with this process? I couldn't stop it happening. I needed to accept it and, with God's help, turn it into a positive and not a negative experience.

In an amazing way colour came to my rescue. As I tried to pray about the 'misery of ageing' this picture came to be.

Because I did not want even to pray about it, it is all on a small scale. I used thin instead of thick felt-tips because even while I did it, I didn't want to look at it. That wasn't a deliberate choice; it just happened.

At first I used only the black, brown and red which are my 'difficult' colours. The brown, I felt, was twisted in all directions. It was the fear I couldn't put into words. The black followed with my depression as I tried to cope with the growing signs of ageing. Would I have to contend with deafness, blindness or loss of mental ability? As I tried to pray to accept such things if they came, I became angry and frustrated instead – hence the red at the centre.

That was as far as I got for a long time. Then I began to see as I prayed that because of the years that had passed – the growth, if you like, of the brown and the black branches – I could be creative in a way that in earlier years had not been possible. I began to see that *because* of age I do have gifts, and if I let them, they can still be used and developed. I was then able to introduce the green shoots and leaves. I had not consciously produced branches when I coloured the brown – just brown ropes entangling me at the centre – but then later I saw that it became a symbolic tree – and what could be more appropriate as a symbol for growth and life? Without the green this was a very sad circle, but now it gives me encouragement and hope. I can trust and be thankful.

We can all find symbols to help us as we look around. We have a mulberry tree that is over 300 years old. It is propped up now and hollow with age, but it still produces a wonderful crop of fruit each year. At any stage of life we can find symbols to help us.

Having shared my circle with you, I hope that you will be encouraged to pray seriously about one of your worries or fears this week. If you put it to the test, you may discover that by using colour as well as words you will be strengthened.

Suggestion

There are so many words of Scripture that can also support and encourage us, but we tend to let them fade.

You might like to choose a verse each day to colour and hang on to. For example:

> Very truly I tell you, unless a grain of wheat falls into the earth and dies it remains alone. But if it dies, it bears much fruit. *John 12:24*

Here are a few references which may be helpful to you:
Psalms 23:4, 27:1, 108:13, 113:4 and 121. Also Matthew 28:20; Luke 6:20, 21; John 14:27, 20:29; Romans 8:38, 39; 1 Corinthians 15.

We have so many promises to hold on to through the years. Find the one that holds you. Let it sink in. You will experience another advent. God does come to us in so many ways.

The Second Week of Advent

Judgement. Don't we all cringe at that word? It has so many negative connections for us, instilled from way back. Too many of us were taught to fear the judgement of God from a very early age. That fear stays with us until we recognise it for what it was – a false conception.

I hated the 'eye' as a symbol of God's presence. I'd been taught that God was watching us all the time and would know if we did anything wrong. What a difference it would have made if we'd been told that God was keeping an eye on us because of his loving concern for each one.

Judgement for many of us conjures up powerful authority figures – ideas not of justice but of punishment being meted out without a shred of mercy or empathetic understanding. We can still find ourselves dreading the judgement of others. We feel nothing we can say can help. In fact, we feel trapped, rather as I felt when I prayed a colour prayer about a situation in which I was caught.

The black trapped me: all my efforts, signified by the purple, made no impression.

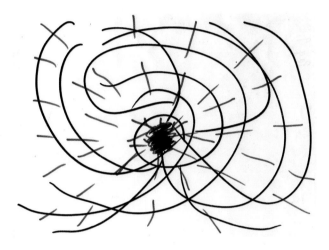

We tend to forget that our Lord's judgement is based on very different criteria from our own. His is not a moralistic code of rules to be obeyed with marks won or lost! Jesus turned our ideas of judgement upside down, and yet we go on turning them the wrong way round again.

Jesus didn't judge the widow in a negative critical way for giving only a mite to the church collection (Mark 12:41-43). Instead he praised her highly for giving all she could. He sees the heart. He did not judge Zacchaeus but loved him into life (Luke 19:1-10). He did the same for Matthew the tax collector (Matthew 9:9) and the woman who kissed his feet while others berated her (Luke 7:36-50). He didn't condemn the woman taken in adultery (John 8:3-11) or the thieves on their crosses (Luke 23:39-43).

We find it very difficult to accept those who cause pain to others, but we can learn to trust and hope in God's love for all. Each and every one of us is accepted. Some of our feelings of lostness are caused by our lack of self-forgiveness, and yet God has freed us, forgiven us and loves us. (Try reading that last sentence with 'me' and 'my' in place of 'us' and 'our.)

Forgiven?

All is past?

The past wiped out? Having no meaning?

No.

The past cannot be denied, only owned and accepted.

The past has made the present.

But the past is in God's safe keeping,

not mine.

I go forward from where I am,

not from where I was.

And God goes with me.

Therein lies forgiveness.

Every forgiveness is another Advent. As we forgive each other, God is in our midst. It is not for us to judge others. God alone knows the full story.

God surrounds everyone's story or struggle with love and understanding. He is in the story.

Purple is a colour which has more than one meaning for me. In this circle it reflects the anxiety which used to swallow me up. (It still has a nibble now and again!)

It is difficult to throw off the worry about 'What will people think?' We judge others but also fear judgement. In fearing someone's judgement we are already judging the other person, expecting unhelpful criticism instead of trusting their motivation, should a difficult remark come our way.

The judgements of Jesus were expressions of love and concern. Are ours? Even Peter wanted to know what was to happen to John (John 21:20-22). It doesn't feel like a caring question but a critical one.

Love is the only criterion by which we are to live. Of course we get things wrong, but we can continue knowing we are held. The Advent of Christ has already been seen so often in our lives through the love shown us by others. As another Advent leads us on, may we prepare our hearts to give as well as to receive love.

Suggestion

I have sometimes kept a diary in colour. Perhaps you would like to try the idea this week. You'll need to draw seven squares and then colour the squares as you look back on each day. You may have an anxious colour, a joyful colour, an angry colour, a peaceful colour . . . Just see what comes. Here are a few such squares that other people have made.

  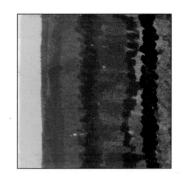

 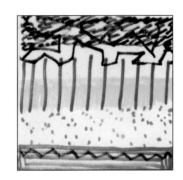 

You'll see that your squares will appear more unified as they will all have been created by one person.

At the end of the week you'll find your squares can tell you much about how God comes to you each day for he is in all colours.

Each square may be a little death and an Advent experience.

The Third Week of Advent

I wonder what your idea of hell might be. As in the case of my thoughts on death and judgement, so my ideas of hell have changed considerably over the years. It is not something or somewhere awaiting those of us who do not measure up to certain standards. No, I believe it's the name given to an experience that I have known in the past, and anyone can experience in the present. Hell may have a different connotation for each one of us but, for me, hell is the state of being in isolation – knowing, or believing, that all relationship with others has been severed to such an extent that one is no longer aware of one's relationship with God. God's love reaches out to us through others – through relationship. It is hard to hang on to the realisation of the reality of our connectedness with God when we are isolated – utterly alone. At such a time it is difficult to express one's longings and emptiness, one's misery.

Even in 'hell', though, there is hope. I found I couldn't not include the purple when I prayed this circle. Here I was thinking of purple as a healing colour. It had to be included. Even in our worst or lowest times we can find that thread from God to hang on to. When we find it almost impossible to trust in God, God trusts us!

Trust

Fear overtook me,
my boat was sinking fast.
I heard no voice but my own.
I saw nothing
and felt nothing
but the force of the storm.

I was unaware of the outstretched arm,
the encouraging voice
that signifies help on hand.
I refused to see him as he entered my boat,
I trusted him no longer.

But he trusted me!
He sank with me
and he lifted me up.

Haven't we all had such moments? Peter must have felt 'in hell' after his threefold denial, but he wasn't left there. He was restored and renewed as we are. God continues to make his Advent known to us at such times.

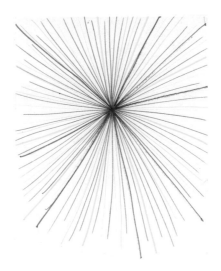

It was this realisation that enabled me to put my 'God colour' behind the previous prayer symbol. Using colour in this way can help strengthen our convictions.

Suggestion

During this week try to pray over your experience of 'hell'. Can you see now that God was with you through those times? Use colour to express your ideas as they come. Yours will be very different from mine. We can only be true to ourselves.

Perhaps you can find more words to help at such times. Hymns can be very supportive and inspiring – for example, 'O love that will not let me go' by George Matheson (1842-1906).

Why not write these, or some other similar words, in a circle and then write your own name at the centre? The message will be emphasised if you add colour to your work.

The Fourth Week of Advent

We have come through to the last week of Advent. We have tried to face our fears – to verbalise or express how we really think of death, judgement and hell.

We have no freedom – we cannot breathe – if we allow ourselves to be swamped by the negative aspects of these subjects. God is not aloof and far removed, and yet we find we so often hesitate to approach him, forgetting that we have his spirit within us. We may need to find a new name for our God.

A new name

Go away!
God of iron, God of rules,
God of stern stuff.
Go away, false God.
Timeless, changeless God.
Rock hard,
righteous God.
'No God' is easier to live with than you have been.

You have misled me.
Fed me on half-truths.
Judgement, but no mercy.
Unobtainable standards
have been my measure.
Love and Forgiveness
not for me.

Fear has been my lot.
Fear of a holiness too 'Holy' to approach.
Too Almighty.

I tiptoed as a child.
Adults daren't even tiptoe.
I keep my distance.

Go away, false God.
Let the real One come.

Let me breathe.
Let me walk upright.
No more shrinking, cowering –
no more paralysis.

New God, real God.
Give me Your Name.
A name in small letters –
no more capitals setting you apart.
What shall I call you?

██████████ is your name.

In ██████████ we can meet.

After giving God a new name I found I had a new lease of life. Spend a little time in finding your own new name with which to greet your God this Christmas, as we join once again throughout the world to accept him into our hearts and lives.

Isn't this what heaven is all about? We do not have to wait for the next life to enter heaven. We have all had glimpses of heaven. For some it has been the moments of deep peace, for others the breathtaking moments of seeing extraordinary beauty or hearing exquisite music.

All of us find heaven in relationships that grow and develop. Heaven is all-inclusive, so that when we once again meet the vulnerability of God in the infant Jesus we can take the whole of ourselves and receive the gifts of life and love.

We can all have our ideas of heaven, but they begin here and now. We miss so much if we shut our eyes to all the advents – the tastes of heaven that come our way.

I'll share with you two of my special times in 'heaven'. One was when I was given a book of drawings by children and young people I had taught in a school in the interior of Sabah, Malaysia. In every picture they had coloured me brown as they were themselves. That was the most loving, accepting gesture they could possibly have made, and the more so as it was completely unconscious. Truly I was in heaven when I saw those pictures for we were all one.

The second vivid memory I have is very different. At one level one could say I was in hell, but it became heaven.

I was on a small cargo boat, crossing the sea between two islands in the Solomons. I love being on the sea and didn't mind the fact that I was the only passenger on deck. As the sky was a little overcast the other passengers had withdrawn.

After a short time, though, the sea became very rough and threw the boat in all directions. I couldn't keep on my feet and was rolling round the deck trying to find something to hang on to. It was an open-sided boat! The two crew members saw my predicament and hauled me up on to a chair. They tied me into the chair and tied the chair to the flagpole. I was safe. I was held tight. I could see the gigantic waves soaring above us as we continued to be tossed around, but the men were experienced sailors and I knew I could trust them to make it to shore.

That was an experience of hell being contained in heaven. Once I believed I was safe, being held to the post, it was an exhilarating experience. We were at one with the elements.

In thinking over that experience I used collage instead of my usual felt-tipped pens.

Occasionally I see a colour that appeals to me even though I may not know why. I cut out this blue from an advertisement in a magazine. I think it was the fact that the blue varies from black to white while still remaining blue. Somehow it reflects how I was feeling while experiencing glimpses of hell and heaven at the same time.

Heaven is wherever God is. As a result I see heaven including all life. Every aspect can be included. This, therefore, is my picture of heaven. It has life, movement and growth – and no colours are excluded.

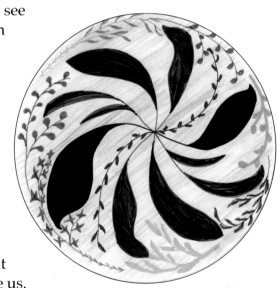

Why not colour your vision of heaven?

Just as every Sunday is a reminder to us of the resurrection, so we can live in the expectation of Christ's coming to us every day.

If we have eyes to see, we shall begin to recognise God's coming in every sign of love. God's love enfolds us and the Spirit of God is within us to strengthen and guide us. Yes, his 'eye' is watching over us to protect and shield us, to keep us safe.

We can get used to such signs, so that they don't touch us any more. Try, therefore, to look at your day-to-day living and see the signs – a kindly word comes your way, a friendly letter, a driver swerves to avoid you, a friend gives you a lift, a child gives you a friendly grin, a baby reaches out to you.

Next week we celebrate Christmas. As the baby Jesus reaches out to us, may we be prepared to reach out to others? The Advent of God needs each one of us in order for his Advent to be complete.

Let's celebrate!